SO! YOU WANT TO BE AN ENTREPRENEUR?

ALSO BY FRED DUFFY
ADVENTURES OF A SERIAL ENTREPRENEUR

SO! YOU WANT TO BE AN ENTREPRENEUR

**Early-stage Critical Advice
From Concept to Cashflow**

FRED DUFFY

SO! YOU WANT TO BE AN ENTREPRENEUR?

Time To Get Moving
This Book will tell you how
50 YEARS SUCCESSFUL STARTUPS
Fred Duffy

The Author

BORN IN 1933, FRED Duffy was raised in Monaghan Town, played football for school and county and was educated in Dublin and Manchester. He qualified as a radio officer in the British Merchant Navy.

During the next 50 years he created a wide range of enterprises; in horticulture where he was voted Businessman of the Year; in the oil industry where he was elected a Fellow of the Institute of Petroleum and built the only privately owned oil recycling plants in Ireland.

Headhunted into a semi state service as a Venture Capital Analyst before an appointment as M.D. of the Irish Health Service Development Corporation. Winning a £20 million contract in Saudi Arabia, he managed a hospital and a regional health service in King Khalid Military City.

The Greenman Group was his last and most expansive business. With plants in three countries, he employed 320, producing computer consumables.

Retiring at 75, he started writing with a memoir which was self-published as 'Adventures of a Serial Entrepreneur' in 2020.

He has written the current book, 'So! You want to be an Entrepreneur?' as a guide and a challenge to school,college leavers and graduates, together with all job seekers to grasp some of the opportunities there for those who are prepared.

To

All school and college leavers, to Graduates and to the many still undecided about their careers, hoping this book helps

and

my lovely wife of 61 years and my extended family.

CONTENTS

INTRODUCTION

WELCOME TO THIS BOOKLET, a guide which may help as you try to decide what to do, to seek employment or to start your own business!

Written for everyone in doubt about their direction in life, school and college leavers together with all job seekers. There are many, in midlife, who may be considering another way for them. Capable and experienced, they are minded to try out a concept that won't go away but lacking in confidence. This guide may help.

Most of what you have learned up to now has been preparing you for this stage. You have. matured and are gaining experience which will have introduced you to a range of possible interests for you to consider.

You are on the cusp of a new chapter of your life. The questions you are facing are serious and I understand the concern you may be experiencing.

I have been there, ...broke, scared – directionless! When I was 16, I failed my exams. My mother, a widow was borrowing money to keep me at college. I didn't know what to do.

Then, I heard about a six-month course that would qualify me for a job as a Radio Officer in the navy. This was something I could do. I borrowed some money, hunkered down and my life changed.

I still remember that period and emphasize with anyone in such a situation.

The good news for you is you are entering a job market with many vacancies. You also have the support of well-informed and enthusiastic local and Government agencies happy to help you. The exciting life in front of you may offer you opportunities you hadn't expected. If you can grasp these with optimism and a positive attitude, you can build a successful, enjoyable future.

I have kept this guide short, but I hope you will find its comparison of different options useful.

In my experience the wide world is full of opportunities you hadn't expected, with room for all our talents. Any decisions you make now will start you on your way, but life is full of twists and turns. That is why I refer to it as an adventure and why I urge you to prepare yourself.

'Luck is when preparedness meets opportunity'. You can be one of the lucky ones.

CHAPTER 1:

ENTREPRENEURS AND MANAGERS

ONE SUMMER EVENING AT a garden party in Surrey I was asked by a young lady what I did for a living.

I tried to explain how my tomato farm had led to an oil-recycling and chemical waste recovery plant but that I was now remanufacturing ink cartridges. She interrupted me and knowingly observed, 'You must be one of those entrepreneurs.'

When I first started earning a living and taking care of my family, I had hardly even heard the word 'entrepreneur'. I just wanted a steady, pensionable job so that I could pay my way with some security. By the time I was 30 I had established such a position in Irish Shell, with an enjoyable job and a defined – if modest – career path.

Then I went and spoiled it all by giving in to a growing desire for challenge and responsibility. I wanted to do my own thing and realized that I would never be content sitting in an office following directives from a faceless administration.

Later in my life I set out to discover the reasons and motivation that had prompted me into a series of start-up ventures, a practice repeated by a number of my children. I decided to find out more about entrepreneurs and how we differ from other managers.

It might be useful if, together, we consider what defines an entrepreneur as distinct from a manager.

Your options are either to secure a position in management with good prospects or risk the entrepreneurial route by creating your own business. I aim to explore the difference between the two.

I should explain, at this stage, that I am a *serial* entrepreneur, who having managed my ventures can justly claim to have an objective view of both positions. I have also written a book about my career which has been commended as a 'great source of inspiration for any budding manager entrepreneur.'[i]

Here are two things to consider:

1. Consider the difference between entrepreneurship and corporate management.
2. Consider your suitability for entrepreneurship. It doesn't suit everyone.

We will review both options together and help clarify your view.

In doing so I will not be too prescriptive about what makes an entrepreneur. We come in all shapes and sizes and cannot easily be defined.

But before we begin, let me ask you two questions.

Why do you want to be an entrepreneur? Why are you reading this book? Why are you playing with the cool title of entrepreneur when you may simply be seeking a good job in corporate business?

I was in my thirties, had worked hard for many years, and was a successful manager before I even heard the word 'entrepreneur'.

The second question: what is the difference between an inventor, a manager and an entrepreneur?

The world of business is run by skilled, disciplined administrators who direct and control our institutions. They are essential executives who ensure the smooth performance of our economy. Nothing I may say in praise of entrepreneurs is intended to belittle the importance of managers.

In one of my jobs, as a business analyst, I interviewed a number of inventors; some with good ideas, most seeking funds to set up and run their own business. Our consensual policy was to package them into a group headed by a business manager.

One morning while on vacation, I visited the Thomas Edison Depot Museum in Port Huron, Michigan, when I was gently challenged by the curator with a rhetorical question. 'I suppose you think Edison was a brilliant inventor?'

He went on to advise me that, "Edison's genius was that if he knew there was a needle in a haystack, he would not stop searching the haystack until he found it. Then he would improve the needle and bring it to market." He continued, "Edison never invented *anything* but identified many objects invented by others which he improved until ready for market."

In my view, Edison was a classical entrepreneur.

Compare him with his friend John D. Rockefeller: neither an inventor nor an entrepreneur but an archetypical manager who built his oil company, Emron, into the largest in the world. Or consider Henry Ford, who didn't invent the car but developed good engineering and mass production, which could produce a car at a price suitable for the average American.

Just think about it. The wide world of business is full of opportunities with room for all our talents. The question is, where do *you* fit?

So let's see if we can answer both questions. This book is written by an artisan who learned his skills on the job and trained a number of young managers to senior and board level. You will not receive an academic essay on the subject, but rather practical questions and suggestions based on fifty years of largely successful entrepreneurial experience. I am hopeful that some of these may help you to answer the questions about what you want and where you might best fit.

Let me be clear: I have no wish to dissuade you from entre-preneurship but I don't want you to see it as the only route to management. If you keep an open mind, I believe that you can learn which route is best suited for you.

Better a fulfilled corporate manager than a frustrated wan-nabe entrepreneur.

CHAPTER 2:

THE DIFFERENCE

SOME COMMENTATORS CLAIM THAT managers and entrepreneurs are of the same breed. I disagree with them.

Let me clarify my strong personal belief that entrepreneurs are a different breed. Our management skills are similar, and entrepreneurs *can* work as managers. When I had an appointment to manage a large hospital in the Middle East, for example, it called for a high standard of management but no entrepreneurship.

It seems to me that the word entrepreneur has been imposed on the title of manager. Anyone managing a small to medium enterprise (SME) is likely to be called an entrepreneur but this inaccurate use of titles in the field of start-up business is misleading.

Most governments have accepted this and have introduced programs that support all start-ups regardless of terminology. The need to promote a positive acceptance by the public and a supportive environment for start-ups by ambitious young businesspeople became a clear objective. Such government programs soon led to the recognition that the singular competences and skills needed for successful SMEs can be learned.

These competences consist of the knowledge and skills you will require to found and grow a successful business. You are advised here to assimilate the required knowledge prior to start-up as well as on the job while you grow the enterprise. As you apply some of these suggested competences your practical skills should gradually strengthen.

Recommended competences:

- communications: clarity, inspiration, networking, ability to pitch
- creativity: initiative, innovation, imagination, outside-of-the-box decision-making: judgement, problem-solving, avoidance of procrastination
- visionary leadership: motivation, engagement, passion, positive mental attitude (PMA), ability to enthuse staff
- management: planning skills, organisation, goal attainment
- strategy; risk assessment, adaptability, curiosity, consumer focus, research, growth
- determination and persistence: accountability, stress management, patience, ability to handle rejections.
- self-confidence: stability, optimism, support for staff, acceptance of criticism and setbacks
- financial: cash flow, cost control, funding, projections, street smarts

Your life experiences will have given you some of these competences and others can be adopted through training and advice from your support programs and mentors. You will not become proficient in all of these overnight but the more you read and study, and are guided, the faster your range of competences and skills will grow.

CHAPTER 3

KNOW YOURSELF

THIS IS WHERE IT gets personal. This chapter is about you: not the product, not the business. That will come later. This is about questions which only you can answer, as frankly and as objectively as possible.

Let me share a little secret about entrepreneurs. As loners, we are mostly introspective. We constantly plan, replan, and evaluate events, ourselves, our performance, and evolving situations. Get used to this. No one will be as interested in you as you are.

Let's get real about how challenging an entrepreneurial career can be. Keep a score sheet as if you were a Special Ops recruit interviewing for active service.

Establish whether you have what it takes for this exacting job.

Rate your answer to every question 0 to 10, as honestly and objectively as you can.

Practical:

1. Are you a leader?
2. Can you sleep well while under mental or physical stress?
3. Are you in good health and keeping fit by using a

gym or other way?

4. Do your family circumstances allow for your being away, often overnight?

Mindset

5. Are you self-confident?
6. Are you mentally strong?
7. Are you tenacious?
8. Are you optimistic?
9. Can you handle the stress of no steady income?
10. Have you a strong PMA?
11. Can you handle loneliness?
12. Are you comfortable with risk?

Interpersonal skills

13. Are you a good judge of situations?
14. Are you streetwise?
15. Are you a good judge of whether people are watching your back?
16. Are you a good communicator?
17. Have you any knowledge of finance, cash flow, costs, margins, budgeting?

You have seen in Chapter 2 what competences and skills are required. Now that you have assessed yourself, how did you score? 170 is the maximum but there is no 'winning score'. The purpose of the quiz is to focus your attention on the requirements for a successful performance in any challenging senior management position. Perhaps the most important questions are numbers 13,14 and 15 which seek to rate your judgement. Your business proposal rests on your judgement.

You must of course realize that this is not a game; this is a personal checklist before you make some life-changing decisions on your next moves. It is a very real and scary challenge to make the decision to start up your own business, to leave a steady and secure job and venture into an uncertain future.

If you are drawn towards an entrepreneurial life you will have no manager to guide you. From now on you are essentially on your own and you must make all decisions alone. It can be a lonely path relying on the security of your plan and on your self-confidence. If you have answered the above questions casually and without due concentration you may be misleading yourself. Think about it and do it again and again until you have no doubt at all. This is a decision you cannot get wrong.

CHAPTER 4:

ARE YOU READY?

'WHEN YOU ACCEPT YOUR self-worth, your self-confidence will allow you to do wonders'

If you have rated yourself well in previous chapters, we can take it that you are positive about your competences and skills, that you trust yourself, and that you value your self-worth. On these values you can carefully build your self-confidence. It is a very real challenge for anyone to make the life-changing decision to start their own business. I built my personal self-confidence step-by-step, using successes in little things to give me the confidence to take that step, but even then it was still scary.

And you need more than self-confidence. You need courage and maturity. It will also depend on your personal circumstances, marriage, family, education, and especially experience.

My immature attempts at starting on my own business are good examples of what not to do. As recounted in Chapter 9 of *Adventures of an Entrepreneur*, I nearly got myself sacked by ill-thought-out and poorly executed initiatives. I was aged 24 at the time, and I hadn't had sufficient experience. By the time I reached 34 and saw a suitable opportunity I had gained a wealth of useful business experience and knowledge.

Albert Einstein's opinion is worth remembering: 'The only source of knowledge is experience.' You need experience to gain knowledge. I am not saying that age is a decisive factor, but I caution you that your personal abilities should be backed up by experience. This will add to your maturity and give you genuine self-confidence based on solid foundations.

Steve Jobs is a prime example.[ii] He created Apple in his twenties, but he was 52 by the time he presented the iPhone. There is much research to confirm the benefits of starting a business at an older age. Harvard, Dukes, and Northwestern Universities have each produced surveys indicating that the average age for start-ups is more slanted towards 40 to 45.

Studies carried out by the National Bureau of Economic Research conclude that 42 has been the average age of 2.5 million founders since 1970. Also, entrepreneurs in this age group are 1.8% more likely to succeed than 30-year-olds. A separate study carried out by Harvard Business School reached similar conclusions. It's worth noting that both studies used the same data, taken from the US Census Bureau.

However, no survey or agency can tell us when it's a good age to start a business or project.

I started my tomato farm aged 35. In 1978 at the age of 45 I started Atlas Oil; in 1992 aged 59 I started the Greenman group; in 2005 aged 72 I opened our factories in Bulgaria. Now in 2023, at 90 I have just launched my third book and am looking forward to writing my magnus opus in the next two years. The general entrepreneurial awareness today has opened up opportunities to all ages, so it is up to you to decide.

Added to experience, I strongly urge you to strengthen your self-confidence with two mental supports that you could adopt as your own. I have used these throughout my business life and have found them most helpful. They are optimism and Positive Mental Attitude, PMA.

Optimism

The Macmillan Dictionary defines optimism as 'a tendency to be hopeful and to expect good things will probably happen.'

There will be times when your will is tested. Things have gone wrong, your business looks like it's failing, your staff are not performing, one of your best staff is dead. There are many problems waiting to threaten your resolve. Optimism will help you through.

The US National Institute of Health summarized fifty-three reports[iii] and concluded:

> It is apparent that optimism is a mental attitude that heavily influences physical and mental health as well as coping with personal goals and development. Optimists are significantly more successful than pessimists in adversity events and when important life goals are impaired.

Winston Churchill[iv] was tested by politics, war and uncertain income, yet he quotes, 'a pessimist sees the difficulty in every opportunity; an optimist sees the opportunity in every difficulty.'

Optimism is a powerful force in our mind which can help us face adversity with resolution and belief that there will be a good outcome. If you're naturally optimistic, focus and build on it. If you're naturally pessimistic you can and should turn this around. Contact Verywell Mind,[v] a partner of the Cleveland Clinic which offers a practical home-based service free of charge to help you become optimistic.

Noam Chomsky[vi] is the world's guru on this subject. His bestseller *Optimism over Despair* is available from Amazon as an audio book. He sums up the subject as follows:

We have two choices. We can be pessimistic, give up and help ensure that the worst will happen. Or we can be optimistic, grasp the opportunities that should exist and maybe help make the world a better place.

'Optimism is the faith that leads to achievement.' Helen Keller[vii]

'I believe that any success in life is made by going into an area with a blind furious optimism.' Sylvester Stallone[viii]

Positive Mental Attitude (PMA)

Referring to *Macmillan Dictionary*'s definition of optimism as a tendency to be hopeful and to expect good things will probably happen, PMA is stronger and more confident, confirming that good things *will* happen for certain.

It is a way of looking at things to face and handle life's setbacks, to approach every situation seeking opportunities for achievement. Partnered by the powerful force of optimism, it seeks and plans for a good outcome in most situations, dismissing negativity and pessimism.

'You have been assigned this mountain to show others how it can be moved.' Mel Robbins

'Being positive in a negative situation isn't naïve, it's leadership.' Ralph Morrison

Optimism combined with PMA can be the bedrock of your self-confidence and will support your leadership skills in the stormy waters you can expect.

CHAPTER 5:

THE ROUTE TO START-UP

'Vision is the art of seeing what is invisible to others.' Jonathan Dean Swift

As you prepare for start-up you are probably on the lookout for a winning idea and ready for the next step. To develop your thoughts or to search for the support you will need as you prepare for your business enterprise.

The problem is where to begin.

As you try to put bones on an idea, you must try to think it out. Your most powerful tool is your brain, an incredible organ that can present and represent your emerging ideas in nanoseconds so you are well-advised to use it. The range of support is useful, so use it when you need to but get ready to do it your way.

It must all start with your idea.

Before you approach any agency I suggest that you start seeking the idea you will bring to market.

This is the hard bit.

You must train yourself to look at *everything* with a fresh pair of eyes and ask why this way? and how another way? How to enhance, to improve, to reduce cost?

To find a winner you need to be imaginative and hungry. You are hunting for an opportunity, a service, a need, a prod-

16

uct. It may already be there but you have an angle to make it, do it, or supply it better. There will always be an opportunity for someone who does things better. It requires observation, research, and skill but most of all, you can benefit from your *curiosity*: why something is being done and how it could be done better. This may be where you discover your entrepreneurial skills. Be patient – encourage your curiosity, perhaps make it a game with a friend. Remember the story about Edison in Chapter 2: opportunities are just waiting to be identified. There are gaps in the market. Watch out for new opportunities with changing demographics and expectations. Make it a habit and after a time it will become ingrained and natural.

With changing demographics there is a growing population of retired older people with an increasing demand for a variety of support services. How about offering a concierge service to them?

Look up sources of business ideas and franchises. One fertile source is your computer. Google keywords, such as 'business ideas', 'start-ups', 'want to start a business but have no money' and so on. You'll be surprised by the volume of ideas and suggestions you'll receive. I urge you to be patient. You are self-training to be an entrepreneur and that's a big task.

You would have an advantage if you select a proposal within your area of expertise. An example of this is the McAllister brothers who started a barber shop in Dublin's prestigious Grafton Street. Seeing a market for a high standard service they adopted a décor which would become standard in future shops. With attractive red ''leather' upholstery and dark mahogany it presented an image and a standard which they franchised as the Grafton Barber. There are currently 52 shops in the group which claims to be the largest chain of family owned barber shops in Europe

Another example is this author; I worked in Shell Petroleum for ten years before I saw a niche opportunity that I could develop. On a personal note we find it difficult to find a GOOD plumber, a GOOD painter, electrician or carpenter.

Another occasion, when I had difficulty finding a project, as I trawled through lists of franchises and books of ideas I found a new opportunity which met all my parameters. It had taken me some months to find, but it was an idea that I knew I could develop. I grew it into the international Greenman Group, employing over three hundred people in five countries.

It was a huge success in a new industry which I may have missed had I not researched the ideas book.

My point? You don't know where or when you will discover the IDEA. You should never stop looking.

What comes next: how about a name?

Pick a name for your proposal. When you are shaping it to present to the world, it will be that much stronger – more real – as if it has its own identity, or emerging brand. Even at an early stage it can help you consider how to develop the idea.

An example is when I was offered a small glasshouse one Sunday in Sligo at a price I couldn't refuse. It was in the wrong place at the wrong time, but it was a real opportunity that I could make work. Time to adapt my plans. Driving back to Dublin that night I shaped my new business. By the time I reached Mullingar, the glasshouses farm would be named Sunnyfresh Nurseries and by journey's end our tomatoes would be branded Top Toms. I had these names before I had even bought the land, but they gave my idea substance that carried conviction as I negotiated bridging finance with the bank.

When you have found a potential winner

Proving the viability and market for a product can call for serious research and cost so I have always used a preliminary simple test which I commend to you. I call it the 'smell test'. Exclude your personal views and objectively check some simple facts.

- Is the market already being supplied?
- Is there room or a need for your proposal?
- Is there a market for your idea?
- If yes, what is the current price? At what price could you deliver it?
- Have you a USP or marketing advantage?
- Is there a latent unserved market?
- What is the market's current size?
- Are there potential routes to market and could you access them?

At about this stage, with the above information and a calculator, you could produce a simplistic overview of profit potential.

If it's lean and mean, forget it. If it's very large check your calculations. But if it smells good it's time to get serious.

Decision time

As an entrepreneur, you have committed to developing a number of skills including strategic planning and decision-making. It is time for those now. You should set aside a period of deep concentration, consider your personal emotions, and try to visualize how the business might evolve.

- Importantly, would you like the business?
- Is it something you would be pleased, even proud to head up?
- Could you see yourself getting enthusiastic about it?
- Would you go it alone or with a partner?

This review may last for days, weeks, or as long as it takes for you to reach a decision.

Be ready for negative reactions. Don't be put off by those who don't share your vision. Their questioning will challenge you to confirm your conviction.

Draft Business Plan

It's now time to draft a business plan. While still at a formative stage you can consider the following headings:

- Operations
- Sales
- Administration
- Personnel
- Finance

Of these, Sales is the most critical. Your success in selling your products will determine the results of your endeavours. Your initial research would have introduced you and your offerings to the market, so test it. Entrepreneurs are often their own best sales staff with their enthusiasm and conviction. Your efforts should reassure you by the reception of the market to your offer. If it's lukewarm it's a signal.

According to CBI surveys the most common reason for failure (42%) is because there is actually no market need for the offering.

You should now be in a Stop/Go position for your proposal. If the market has signaled 'NO', it's time for a rethink. If 'GO', it's time to seek advice and support from enterprise advisors.

Any person with a good proposal anywhere in Ireland should have little difficulty in securing support by way of a government agency. The agency you approach will depend mainly on where you live. Let's assume that you live in Northern Ireland.

Northern Ireland

The authorities here are committed to providing every start-up with a range of support and advice on how to progress. Training programmes are available for all ages, but some are fairly basic introductions to the commercial world. One you might find useful is 'My Money Matters' which can help beginners with planning their cash flows.

There are two main support agencies.

Your first contact might be nibusinessinfo.co.uk which includes a free online service with a step-by-step guide, 'My New Business'. It offers mentor guidance with a telephone line to make contact and seek advice on issues such as clarifying your proposal, potential problems, goal setting, and access to financial support including grants, loans, and equity support. Importantly it also guides you on legal and corporate matters and on practical details such as location, premises, and organization. The phone line is 0800 1814422.

Another route is Enterprise Northern Ireland which can guide you to your nearest Local Enterprise Agency. This is a network of twenty-seven local agencies in sixty-six locations over eleven council areas. There are 148 local business advisors, knowledgeable and eager to support you, especially in the early stages. Their services to SMEs include monthly updates on grant incentives and finances with preferential access to relevant learning for you and your team.

Other support

- Ni Direct (https://www.nidirect.gov.uk/).
- 'Go For It' advises on business plans.
- Border People advises people who move across the NI border (https://borderpeople.info/).

- The Prince's Trust provides training, mentoring and financial assistance to young entrants aged between 18 and 30 (https://www.princes-trust.org.uk/).
- UK StartUps advertises government funds currently available (https://www.ukstartups.org/).
- Business Plan Review provides government funding for SMEs
- Start Your Own Business helps businesses in Northern Ireland (https://syob.net/uk).
- Business Intelligence Center provides businesses with access to market and industry information (www.CBINSIGHTS.com). According to CBIsights, a top-rated intelligence platform, the second reason for startups' failure, 35%, is because there is no need for the offering. The first reason at 36% is due to the runout of cash.
- Invest Northern Ireland (https://www.investni.com/)
- Startups (https://startups.co.uk/)
- Entrepreneur Handbook: guide to grants, technology, marketing, legal etc (https://entrepreneurhandbook.co.uk/).
- http://smallbusiness.co.uk/; https://www.startuploans.co.uk/; https://www.simplybusiness.co.uk/

InterTradeIreland: phone +44 28 3083 4100. From the old Gas Works Business Park in Newry, United Kingdom, InterTradeIreland (ITI) has been helping SMEs for over two decades. A joint North–South body established under the 1998 Belfast Agreement, it operates Enterprise Support Programmes to assist SMEs with growth, building capacity, research, and innovation among other things.

Their services offer support with funding and business insight for SMEs throughout the island of Ireland who are trying to grow their business. Start-up businesses that innovate and do things differently are more likely to expand and grow. When extra specialist expertise is advised ITI can help access specialists and provide financial support for young businesses.

ROI Government

The Republic of Ireland has a clear policy: 'The continued growth of our economy is highly dependent on entrepreneurs and the SMEs that they create.' Under a 'Programme For Government – Our Shared Future', a SME taskforce of entrepreneurial business leaders was established to prepare an ambitious long-term plan for the development of the entrepreneurial and SME sector. This includes measures to assist start-ups to scale up, enhance their digital capabilities, and increase export activities. This plan has resulted in a range of support for young enterprise in Ireland, including funding opportunities, networking opportunities, and accelerators.

Enterprise Ireland

Phone +353 1 727 2000
This is the state agency for supporting the development of all businesses in Ireland but especially large businesses. It provides funding and support for large companies who are expanding their activities and exporting their goods and services. It also supports enterprises and entrepreneurs with high potential for rapid start-ups.

Importantly it also supports the efforts of SMEs through a network of local enterprise offices.

Local Enterprise Offices

Known as LEOs, these are the local access branches of Enterprise Ireland. They form a network of thirty-one regional support centres that combine the expertise of Enterprise Ireland and the broad reach of local authorities. The network caters for small- and medium-sized enterprises seeking support to grow their business and trading in the domestic market. Their role is to drive the development of local enterprise, putting local small and micro enterprises at the heart of job creation in Ireland. They support businesses and start-ups, and promote a 'can do' business attitude. They increase the job potential of new and existing small businesses and the number of innovative businesses with potential for growth. Additionally they can provide a pathway for suitable firms to be accepted by Enterprise Ireland for opportunities to export.

They also provide mentoring, training, and management development programs overseen by Enterprise Ireland. They give access to a range of support services including planning, licensing, and importantly, access to the Microfinance Ireland Loan Fund.

They are staffed by positive and knowledgeable executives who have a number of schemes focused on helping SMEs.

- For start-ups, the most useful support is probably the Feasibility/innovation Grant which can help you with researching the market and viability of your concept.
- There is also the Online Trading Scheme, aimed at helping you expand sales by easing you into trading online.
- At a later stage but within your first eighteen months there is the Priming Grant; in effect, a start-up grant.
- Later, the Business Expansion Grant can help you expand your business.

The LEO framework organizes a Local Enterprise Week each year to promote general interest in business and specifically to simulate your ambition, your online training, productivity, planning for exports, and more.

Another occasion organized by the LEO network is the NWED, the National Women's Enterprise Day. LEOs also run the annual National Enterprise Awards which highlight successful businesses around the country.

If you are planning to start up in the Republic, you need have little doubt that your local LEO should be your first-stop shop.

Other supports:

- Think Business, Bank of Ireland
- microfinanceIreland.ie/startups.ir
- LinkedFinance: start-up loans
- Inland Revenue: rebate of income tax from previous six years
- Newfrontiers.ie
- Inspiredstartups.com
- Dublin BIC
- Thinkbusiness.ie
- Mentors-work.ie
- Isme.ie: Irish SME association
- SBCI, Strategic Banking Company Ireland. Offers low-cost credit to Irish SMEs.

Faced with such a broad range of government and business support, you will need much research and discussion to determine which may suit you best. Your choice will be important as it will largely determine how quickly you can bring your new business into being.

CHAPTER 6

MANAGING YOUR CREATION

By now you will have plugged into the support system of your choice with an approved business plan and an agreed corporate structure.

I have been there several times and I'm pleased to share with you the story of how I took my first steps, that got me off the ground within a limited capital budget. You may find it useful.

Before you start your business, it is advisable to organize it in your mind, to shape it and decide on your aspirations and personal objectives. Do you intend the business to be a lifetime operation which you can sell or pass on to your family? Would you prefer to grow it into a medium-sized operation with continuing growth? The problem with staying small is that your competitors may outgrow you, cut prices, and put you out of business.

Another question you should face early in the life of the business is what type of manager you intend to be. Are you going to be relaxed, allowing the business to be run by the operatives, or are you a strong leader, shaping and deciding its direction?

It is harder to manage a small business than a medium-sized one. Small means that you must multitask to cover all aspects of the company. In the early critical phase of the infant business there is a certain urgency. You will be responsible for the supply chain, sales, distributors, personnel, professional support, and most importantly you will have full financial control.

It sounds a lot, and it is.

But it's manageable, if you take it step-by-step and focus on priorities.

Bottom Line

After all your planning it's important to remember that your reason for trading is to make a profit, so that your trading accounts will always produce a satisfactory bottom line.

Cash flow

Sometimes your costs could submerge your accounts if you miss urgent demands. The real secret of successful trading is control of cash flow, the lifeblood of the business.

With the above priorities in mind, I have always focused on and prioritized the following simple and functional outline structure.

- sales
- cost control
- staff
- operations
- administration including finance

Sales deserve priority as they generate the required margin of profit although challenged by the need to control costs as overheads grow.

The staff are the backbone and infrastructure of the organization.

Operations include everything that moves, supply chain, production, premises and staff performance.

On top of this is administration, which is your responsibility. I have shown finance in brackets as it can be outsourced in the early months.

Sales and Marketing

You should promote your sales with every tool possible: SEO, telesales, blogging, mailshots. If you are a natural salesperson and you have a good backstory, tell it to your market, use the local radio and newspapers. They love a good story about new jobs, planned expansion; good news for their listeners and readers.

Sales do not always flourish and should be supported by a defined marketing strategy which requires you to promote a marketing plan. Preparing a plan is a discipline that encourages you to research markets and the competition. It also forces you to think deeply about your product and its place in an ever-changing market. Advice on this complicated area, including templates and more, can be sourced from a number of agencies such as Fiverr, Upwork, Atlasian, Openstax, and others.

Staff

This is where your drive and charisma come in. Your 'wild spirit', the strength of your vision, must enthuse your staff and commit them to your team. All employees will look to you for strong leadership and a secure business model which for them means a secure job. They also expect good conditions of employment. But there is more. Their performance will be enhanced in a positive atmosphere of enthusiasm, the confidence of a winning, caring team and boss. According to CBI insights, 23% of small business failures are due to a lack of interest and poor teamwork in the workplace. You may not have time for conversation with every individual but a few words showing your interest will go a long way. As chairman of a company with over two hundred employees, I was affectionately referred to as the 'old man'.

The spin-off from your efforts can be surprising. In addition to good overall performance by the general staff it can also increase the ambitions of the higher achievers to the point where they can develop into group leaders, foremen and managers. You may also establish a good reputation for your business as a nice place to work. I once received a call from a competitor recommending a good worker who was moving to our town; he also recommended *us* to the worker. We hired him and he quickly became a foreman. After a year he was a manager.

Human resource management is an important and legal professional area. It will require a high amount of your personal attention and interest until the business can afford a Personnel Supervisor.

On a personal note, as owner-manager you are essentially on your own. You may have mostly good days, but problems do arise to stress you. It is important therefore to keep fit and healthy, especially with a positive mindset, a PMA. The adage that the glass is half-full is misleading; it is sometimes empty and will require you to metaphorically refill it.

Operations

As soon as your business grows beyond a 'one man band', the area of operations will need your attention.

Materials purchase and production together with quality and quantity control will be important. Ancillary to this are storekeeping, logistics and dispatch.

As general manager, you'll need to clarify areas of responsibility, lay down procedures, and appoint and train staff for these functions. As the company grows these appointees must be supported and developed.

This is where mentors can prove very helpful.

Administration

Your creation has grown, and you are a general manager, charged with all administration. Other responsibilities include control of property, adherence to government regulations, insurances, policies, disciplinary matters, and appointing senior management. It also includes finance, initially outsourced until you appoint a financial supervisor.

You will now need a personnel supervisor who can relieve you of considerable responsibility.

All of the above can happen iteratively and without much drama, provided that you are in regular control.

I have done this four times in my career and found it very fulfilling.

You can do it too.

CHAPTER 7:

THE LONG HAUL

WHEN YOU ARE EMPLOYING ten or more, with turnover reaching towards €1,000,000 and upwards, it is time to take stock of yourself, your business, and where you wish to go from here.

It is an exciting time: your business is growing. This is where you had hoped to be and various options are beginning to appear. Depending on the strength of the market, you may decide to continue growing organically. If planning on this route, you might consider offering some equity or even seats on your Board to committed managers.

Outside interests may intrude into your planning at any stage; for example overtures from larger companies seeking entry, sometimes offering equity or investment packages which may not be attractive or properly valued. Such approaches can be aggressive or not, but either way will give you pause. They may divert you from your business plan and they will test your judgement of people and situations.

Equally, some agencies may wish to encourage your growth by acting as a matchmaker, with similar effects. Or you may personally be attracted by some options from investors to provide resources for you to expand by acquisition. A larger operation could support professional management to share your responsibility and strengthen your company in order to repel aggressive takeovers.

As your business profile grows you must be prepared to defend yourself and your business. Note: carefully maintain your majority of voting rights on the board. Problems will occur and you must always watch your back. Some staff may steal from you, perhaps go to a competitor, or simply start up in business against you. There will always be employee problems, illness, and even deaths so be ready for the unexpected.

Additionally, you need to watch out for potentially complex situations. Unexpected problems can arise from extraneous circumstances such as currency variations, change of government policies, bank strikes, transport strikes, or Brexit and the Covid pandemic which virtually closed the economy. You may risk your business or miss opportunities if you aren't prepared to take action or aren't suitably prepared to turn difficulties into opportunities. The fallout from a bank strike or Brexit will have created such opportunities for those who had planned for it. 'A good plan well-executed now is better than a better plan next week.' General Patton.

These and similar situations will provide you with opportunities to show your leadership to your staff and others. It's very easy to get comfortable and let new opportunities drift right by. Now that your business is well-established and resourced, it is an opportunity to revisit your entrepreneurship and direct your company towards new opportunities.

While still in the growth phase this might be a good time to consult a mentor. The Local Enterprise Office will have a number of mentors for you to consider. Your trust in a mentor will require the right chemistry as well as patience as they learn your business, and you both build respect for each other.

Taking advice from the LEO, you should establish what a mentor could offer you and whether you are ready to work with one. Confirm what they bring to the business bring to the business. They are neither employees nor investors with their remuneration or contract to be advised by the LEO.

Sometimes you'll get low and be required to bring out your entrepreneurial spirit to raise morale and reassure your team. You can do this positively by assessing the good things in your business: you're doing what you wished for in a business you created. You are living your dream.

Let me share with you an example of how this works. On one occasion when I was recovering from a heart attack, I hired a CEO to run the business. He looked good on paper but three of the management team – all directors – approached me rather diffidently to say they were going to resign. They loved their jobs but they were dismayed that our company was losing out to the competition because of the lack of enthusiasm and leadership by the CEO.

Unless I took back full control they couldn't see a future. He had to go.

I agreed, took back full control, managed the CEO respect-fully and proceeded with the rest of the company as follows. Firstly, I called a general meeting of all the staff in our main fac-tory in Epsom, about a hundred. I was talking to my directors through the staff as I enthused them with good plans for the coming quarter. By coincidence, the next week would be the Diwali holiday. If we made a push to increase production, we would have a celebratory party. It worked. I enthused myself, my team, and my operatives. Production and morale went up.

I was and am so grateful to those three directors who pressed me to take action.

Much of the above is weighted towards problems but of course there are many high points; successes both financial and strategic. If you are expanding into the export business either in sales or facilities you have the powerful introduction of the LEOs and the even more powerful agency of Enterprise Ireland.

There is also a little-valued element in business called 'luck'. We plan on the setbacks but we shouldn't overlook the part that luck can play. See Appendix 2, 'Luck'.

Let me remind you of the quotation by the twenty-year boss of Walt Disney films, Bob Iger: 'What I really learned over time is that optimism is a very, very important part of leadership.' It is my sincere hope that this, and perhaps some other thoughts in these pages, will help sustain your courage and your *unternehmergeist* for the long haul.

CHAPTER 8:
CONCLUSION

WHATEVER CAREER YOU ARE leaning towards at this time, I believe that you'll have learned important things about yourself.

You will have recognized your abilities and your strengths. Hopefully you have progressed towards the self-confidence and optimism that will help you through the travails of business, whichever route you choose.

If you are leaning towards self-employment and possible entrepreneurship, you'll have broadened your awareness of the challenges that await you and will enter the fray with no cosmetic illusions.

If you are thinking that self-employment is not your choice, you'll have grown to accept your own worth, a worth that has a lot to contribute to some lucky employer.

And if you have come to no defined conclusion, that's all right too. Life is about growing, and this is what you're doing. We don't always know where we're going or where we'll end up. Keep this book and refer to it when you want to. Keep thinking, keep trying, and prove yourself to yourself every day.

One day you'll be where you belong, successful and fulfilled.

My warmest regards to you on your journey

SO! YOU WANT TO BE AN ENTREPRENEUR? REVIEWS

"It's very enjoyable and informative; a thought provoking read".
> Ciara Loughney
> Head of Programmes
> Christian Aid
> Dublin

For any motivated employee considering a foray into business, this book provides a brilliant experience-based framework for getting serious about your idea. From theoretical guiderails to action, Duffy's book is the next step if you're. seeking guidance from someone in your corner rooting for your success.

Don't pass up this ember, It may be the spark that lights your fire.
> Thomas Ruschke, Sales Manager
> Munich

This booklet is full of hard-earned wisdom. In something that's often overlooked in similar books (I've read a few!) -the author takes time to make the comparison between careers in management and entrepreneurship. He shows how easy it is to have unrealistic expectations about the entrepreneurial route and provides a sobering alternative perspective that all who are interested be becoming an entrepreneur should read. Best thing is in a time-poor world - it's an easy read in less than an hour.

Sinead McCaughey
CEO
Yogandha Ltd
Dublin

Excellent contribution to our world of teaching.

Is this short book fit for purpose? Definitely.

A manual that every student of business and every investor venturing into business should read before they start.

This book will ensure a razor sharp focus on the practical outcome of a business course for anyone making a career change into the world of business.

Nicola Browne , M.D.
Mighty Oak, Essex
Giving every child a voice

I really enjoyed Duffy's. SYWTBAE. It's fascinating. I loved the idea of developing better systems of doing things and wish I'd known it was a marketable skill. The author says. "There will always be an opportunity for someone who does things better". As a Montessori teacher, I gave children opportunities to explore and develop their own paths to success.

I also love the idea of asking why? Why does this work? Why not? Will this work better? No one teaches this to kids.

My favorite quote. "Being positive in a negative situation is not naive, It's leadership".

This book deserves every success.

Niamh Wallace
President
Inner Wheel
Dublin

So! You want to be an Entrepreneur' provides a refreshingly practical approach to building a successful business, emphasising the need for planning at every stage, of self-preparedness, of self confidence, of product us, of production and perseverance.

Duffy introduces his fast track "Concept to Cashflow", which encourages entrepreneurs with practical tips such as his 'smell test' to quickly evaluate potential margins on possible planned products or services.

The book is packed with real-world examples from Duffy's experience in successfully launching and driving three international companies.

Whether you're a seasoned trader or just starting out, 'this is a valuable reference for anyone who wants to build or manage a successful business with the least amount of risk and the greatest chance of success.

Dalila Allegra. Finance Director
Lisbon and London

For my review. I can only say. Congratulations and well done. You have touched on so many important points of entrepreneurship and being self-employed. Furthermore, the practical tips you provide can be invaluable for any startup. The questions you want them to ask themselves and the areas that you touch are spot on.

I am sure your book could help a lot of people in making a more informed decision on what to do about their life. I look forward to seeing it in print.

Andrea Gattrimger, Executive Director
Ehrendorf, Austria*Booklife* review

APPENDIX 2:

LUCKY IN BUSINESS

IN THE TOUGH WORLD of business we are prepared to take the setbacks but tend to dismiss a turn of events that could be defined as lucky.

We should not always dismiss this feature of life in our careers. Of course we can't depend on being lucky, but one can be prepared to avail of any lucky opportunities that occur.

'LUCK is what happens when preparation meets opportunity.' Roman philosopher Seneca.

The comment 'he was just lucky' is derisory of one's achievements, implying that favorable circumstances accounted for one's success rather than one's ability.

It was this derisory term that annoyed both Napoleon and Eisenhower. Napoleon's view was, 'Ability is of little value without opportunity. I would rather my generals be lucky than able.' His point was that he knew his generals were able and if opportunities were to occur, they would be lucky.

Eisenhower made a similar point: 'I'd rather have a lucky general than a smart general. They win battles.' He could speak with authority as he had several of the best US generals in history under his command. General Patton was a most successful soldier who didn't believe in luck. His motto: 'There is no such thing as luck, merely opportunity meeting preparedness.'

One of the most spectacular incidents of luck gave Eisenhower his moment in history. On June 5th, the eve of the planned invasion of Europe, the Allies had assembled after months of preparation the largest ever invasion force: 7,000 ships, 12,000 aircraft, 200,000 sailors and 133,000 troops, all tied down by very bad weather. Timing was critical but if the assault were attempted in the fierce gale, it was likely to be a disaster. A sudden call came from the weather team: 'A 24-hour good weather window, tomorrow. Yes, we're sure.' Eisenhower made the decision, gave the order, and on June 6th, D-Day was launched.

Luck is defined by dictionary.com as the force that seems to operate for good or evil in a person's life as in shaping circumstances. Over a fifty-year career I have seen the benefits of luck on several occasions. For example, as I mentioned earlier, when a competitor in Birmingham phoned me to recommend a technician who was relocating to London, he also recommended my company to the technician. This morphed into a successful conclusion for both parties, the technician becoming a manager in my company within twelve months. Was that luck, or preparedness meeting opportunity?

Or another example: after ten years of research and development, I produced a recycled oil to sell into a $5 per barrel market, which was suddenly hit by the Yom Kippur War. This was followed by a series of disputes which drove the price of oil up to $40 per barrel and made us a fortune. Was that luck, or good fortune?

But when I tried my luck at the Blackjack table in Las Vegas, Lady Luck left the room and I lost my float within twenty minutes.

Chris Wong, CEO of Cloudfare, Singapore, says, 'Luck plays a big part in success. I believe that the harder you work the luckier you get. Of course having good Feng Shui at your desk also helps.'

REFERENCES

i   https://www.amazon.co.uk/Adventures-Serial-Entre-preneur-Achievements-Adversity-ebook/dp/B08LMXS96J

ii   Steve Jobs. Born in 1955 and died in 2011, aged only 56. He was victim to pancreatic cancer which he tried to self-treat for nearly a year, until it was too late. Always a techie, always thinking outside the box, he approached the HP boss while still a teenager and suggested an addition to their range. Bill Hewlett offered him a job.

Some time later he met Steve Wosniak and after attending an electronic course they both decided to manufacture their own computer. Starting in Jobs' garage in 1976, they produced their first ever computer in 1977. Entrepreneurs are not easy bedfellows, and he left the partnership in 1985.

When he returned in 1997 they were really ready to roll. Over the next twelve years they changed the world, producing the iMac, the iPod, the iPhone, and the iPad. There will always be a question as to how much more he might have contributed if he had lived longer.

iii   US National Inst of Health: 'Optimism may add a few extra years to one's life', July 15, 2022. According to research published in the Journal of the American Geriatric Society.

iv   Winston Churchill, British politician. Quote source: Restore.org.uk, 21 May 2020.

v   Verywellmind is one of the largest mental health sites in the world. It has about 150 million users each year putting it in the top ten health information sites. With the slogan 'Know more, live brighter', this is a pleasantly presented mental health resource supported by hundreds of experts and partnered by the Cleveland Clinic. It will certainly help readers to be optimistic and much more if required.

vi   Noam Chomsky is a controversial expert in language, politics, and philosophy; a theoretical linguist whose work treated languages as a uniquely human biological and cognitive capacity. His view on how language and the human brain developed, and how it is arguably what makes the human brain cognitively distinct from other creatures, is controversial. He is outraged by the activities and the pernicious influence of the economic elite on domestic policy, foreign policy, and intellectual culture. He believes that all information should be public.

vii   Helen Keller was born in June 1880 and was struck by a high fever in her second year, leaving her deaf and blind. She was taught how to communicate through Braille and lipreading by a wonderful teacher. Her courage and fight to overcome disability turned her into a celebrity both as a writer and in films about her life.

viii   Sylvester Stallone is a film star who mostly portrays a strong dominant character.

INTERACTIVE LECTURES

So! You Want to be an Entrepreneur?

Watch out for Tutorials. To Be Advertised

ALSO

Confidential Consultations.

Printed in Great Britain
by Amazon

38786789R00036